Prophetic Musings

31 Days of Reflection, Prayer, and Intercession

Carol M. BoRich
Artistic impressions by Zoey Rosenthal

Prophetic Musings: 31 Days of Reflection, Prayer, and Intercession
First Edition, 2020
Copyright © 2020 by Carol M. BoRich

All rights reserved. No part of this publication may be reproduced, stored in a retrieval system, or transmitted in any form by any means—electronic, mechanical, photocopy, recording, or otherwise—except for brief quotations in critical reviews or articles, without the prior permission of the publisher, except as provided by U.S. copyright law.

Scripture quotations marked (KJV) are from The Authorized (King James) Version. Rights in the Authorized Version in the United Kingdom are vested in the Crown. Reproduced by permission of the Crown's patentee, Cambridge University Press.

Scripture quotations marked (MSG) are taken from *THE MESSAGE*, copyright © 1993, 2002, 2018 by Eugene H. Peterson. Used by permission of NavPress. All rights reserved. Represented by Tyndale House Publishers, a Division of Tyndale House Ministries.

Scriptures marked (NKJV) taken from the New King James Version®. Copyright © 1982 by Thomas Nelson. Used by permission. All rights reserved.

Scripture quotations marked (NLT) are taken from the Holy Bible, New Living Translation, copyright ©1996, 2004, 2015 by Tyndale House Foundation. Used by permission of Tyndale House Publishers, a Division of Tyndale House Ministries, Carol Stream, Illinois 60188. All rights reserved.

Scripture quotations marked (TPT) are from The Passion Translation®. Copyright © 2017, 2018 by Passion & Fire Ministries, Inc. Used by permission. All rights reserved. ThePassionTranslation.com.

To order additional books:
www.amazon.com
www.BoRichMinistries.com

ISBN: 978-1-7332679-7-7

Editorial and Book Packaging: Inspira Literary Solutions, Gig Harbor, WA
Book and Cover Design: Brianna Showalter, Ruston, WA
Illustrations/Artistic Impressions: Zoey Rosenthal
Printed in the USA by Ingram Spark

In loving memory of

Janice E. Lewis

*my BFF and
the epitome of
God's love*

For wisdom will come from my mouth;
words of insight and understanding
will be heard from the musings of my heart.
Psalm 49:3, TPT

Table of Contents

Foreword vi

How to Use This Book 1

Introduction 3
1 Where You Are 6
2 Carnival 12
3 Signs 17
4 Cutting Horse 22
5 The Classroom 28
6 Crawlspace 32
7 Oyster Bed 36
8 Ah-Ha Moment 41
9 Woodstock 45
10 Valley of Decision 50
11 Dam 55
12 Vineyard 60
13 Passage 65
14 Birthday 70
15 Apartment 75

Table of Contents

16 Duck 80
17 Fog 85
18 Shout 89
19 Ocean Liner 93
20 Music 97
21 Cloak 101
22 Honeycomb 106
23 IV Drip 111
24 Sheep Dip 115
25 Picket Fence 119
26 Puzzle 123
27 Sandcastle 128
28 The Big Game 134
29 Storm 139
30 Fan 143
31 Scope 147

About the Author 153
Contact 155

Foreword

It still amazes me to consider that God, the eternal, infinite, and indescribably majestic God of the universe, speaks to us—people. But He does, and He takes great delight to do so.

From the very beginning of creation, God talked with Adam and Eve and they with Him. People are designed to hear from God. This is perfectly normal in God's design.

Not only is God talking to people very real, it is practical. God desires to protect and direct. He wants to encourage, strengthen, and edify. God yearns to nurture relational intimacy with His people.

In her book, Carol shares some of the times and ways that God has spoken to her. She desires for you to be encouraged, strengthened in your faith, and challenged in the fact that God also speaks to you.

Carol takes seriously the privilege that God speaks; she consistently lives listening to Him, and she graciously ministers to others sharing God 's heart and mind for them. As one of her pastors, I have watched Carol live this out with integrity.

Enjoy Carol's book, read it meditatively, and listen for God to speak to you as you read it.

Mike Riches
Pastor

How to Use This Book

These dreams and visions that I've experienced during my own times of prayer with the Lord have been written and drawn to the best of our abilities—mine and my illustrator— to relay what we believe to be the heart of God in them.

As you read them and meditate on the scriptures provided, be sensitive to what the Spirit may be speaking to you. I've left blank lines in each section—"Your Musings"— for you to write your impressions and reflections, as the Holy Spirit leads you.

After considering the prophetic musing in light of the scriptures provided, and the prayer, record your impressions of what the Holy Spirit might be speaking to you personally. I pray your spirit is touched in profound ways as to the magnitude of the love of the Lord towards you!

Introduction

"Wake up!" came the voice in the night. "Write the book!"

I knew exactly, even at 2:00 a.m., what this meant. For years, it had been prophesied over me that I would write a book. I always thought that if I did, it would be a book about my very colorful life and testimonies. Not this time. The players in this book are you (my reader), our Father God, Jesus, and the Holy Spirit. My part is only to relay the Father's heart to you through the dreams and visions I've received over the years—some on quiet cliffs overlooking the Okanogan Valley, some while tucked in the arms of the Spirit during sleep or prayer, and some in the most of mundane of places, like while on my knees washing my kitchen floor.

I have deliberately left this compilation of impressions without direct interpretation because I wanted to leave room for the Spirit to speak to you, too, though the scriptures and intercessory prayers I've included along with each one give some direction of intention.

I hope you'll take them one at a time, perhaps one a day for thirty-one days. Please muse on each chapter and glean from the richness of the Spirit. The Father's heart is in each reflection, with the intention of drawing you closer to Him.

Carol M. BoRich
Gig Harbor, Washington
March 2020

Prophetic Musings

1

Where You Are

IN THE SPIRIT

I was standing on a hill overlooking a city at night, a city the size of Las Vegas. The tall buildings were all lit up and the streets were busy. The hustle and bustle were alluring; I wanted all it had to offer!

I was in love with a man from this city and was awaiting his wedding proposal. In that instant, as I looked upon the city, I was told by a friend that the man was not interested in me. I had a deep sense of rejection and my heart felt void.

Then from behind me I heard a voice saying, " Your Betrothed is here for you!" My heart leaped in passionate joy and I wept profusely and profoundly as I sensed the nearness of the Beloved. I couldn't turn around and face Him. He said to me, "Turn around my beloved; your shame is gone."

I turned to see an average-looking man, a man with whom I was now so enormously and passionately in love, to the depths of my being. All thoughts of the other melted away. I cried on and on in deep yearning. I asked Him what religion He was, and He threw back His head and roared with laughter.

The scene faded and another came into my view. We were now standing together in the midst of a village of dirt roads, shacks, and utter barrenness. In the streets, I saw children in brightly colored clothes, running and playing. My Beloved said to me, " Will you come with me, no matter where I go or what it looks like? Will you be with me forever?"

I wailed deeply out of the immense love I had for Him and said, "Yes, Lord, anything; I just want to be where you are." We walked on, not looking back.

IN THE WORD

1 John 2:16, TPT

For all that is in the world, the lust of the flesh, and the lust of the eyes, and the pride of life, is not of the Father, but is of the world.

2 Kings 6:19, KJV

And Elisha said unto them, "This is not the way, neither is this the city; follow me, and I will bring you to the man whom ye seek."

Isaiah 30:21, NLT

Your own ears will hear him. Right behind you a voice will say, " This is the way you should go," whether to the right or to the left.

Song of Songs 1: 5b, TPT

I know I am so unworthy, so in need. "Yet you are so lovely!"

Song of Songs 5:4, TPT

My beloved reached into me to unlock my heart. The core of my very being trembled at His touch. How my soul melted when He spoke to me.

Luke 14:26, TPT

When you follow me as my disciple, you must put aside your father, your mother, your wife, your sisters, your brothers—yes, you will even seem as though you hate your own life. This is the price you'll pay to be considered one of my followers.

· · · · ·

PRAYER

Lord, I just want to be where You are. All that the world has to offer is bleak and transient. There's no security there—no hope, no true love—and its ways are dark and mischievous. I take pleasure in knowing that the world rejects me; it rejected You. I don't want to be like the things of the world. I am empty and void without You.

But then, I hear a voice calling me! It's You! I want Your true love, Your everlasting, unconditional love. I want all that You are and I'm willing to pay any price, even forsaking all the world has to offer. Your voice causes me to weep with such longing for You. You have reached my core and I tremble and melt within to be where You are. No matter what the cost, I'm in. I choose to follow You now and forever. Thank You, Lord; I love you so. Amen.

2

Carnival

IN THE SPIRIT

I saw a brightly colored carnival; the entrance had a tall entryway with a sign that read, "The Carnival of Problems and Concerns." The gate was open and there was no fee to enter. It was all free.

To the left and right were booths with different "vendors" and games. I walked in the aisle between them. I saw a booth with a sign that read, "Health," another that said, "Family," then "Job," and many other booths. I continued on down the aisle, amazed at the crowds. Here and there, people would stop and play the game at a particular booth, becoming totally engrossed and desperately trying to beat the odds and win.

At the end of the long aisle between the booths was another large gate, an exit. On the outside of the carnival gate was a throne of gold and jewels. Jesus was sitting on the throne, holding a staff and wearing a crown. He called out to the game players to come to Him outside of the carnival and be with Him at His throne. But the carnival was so distracting, so enticing, that few went to visit Him.

· · · · ·

IN THE WORD

Numbers 20:17, NKJV
Please let us pass through your country. We will not pass through fields or vineyards, nor will we drink water from wells; we will go along the King's Highway; we will not turn aside to the right hand or to the left until we have passed through your territory.

Jeremiah 17:12, NKJV
A glorious high throne from the beginning is the place of our sanctuary.

Ezekiel 43:1-2, NKJV
Afterward he brought me to the gate, the gate that faces toward the east. And behold, the glory of the God of Israel came from the way of the east.

Ezekiel 43:7, NKJV

The Lord said to me, "Son of man, this is the place of my throne and the place where I will rest my feet. I will live here forever among the people of Israel."

Psalm 9:9, NKJV

The Lord also will be a refuge for the oppressed, a refuge in times of trouble.

Psalm 145:18, NKJV

The Lord is near to all who call upon Him, to all who call upon Him in truth.

Matthew 11:28, NKJV

Come to Me, all you who labor and are heavy laden, and I will give you rest.

Mark 4: 19, NKJV

. . . and the cares of this world, the deceitfulness of riches, and the desires for other things entering in choke the word, and it becomes unfruitful.

1 Peter 5:7, KJV

. . . casting all you care upon Him, for He cares for you.

I Thessalonians 5:24, NKJV

He who calls you is faithful, who also will do it.

PRAYER

In this moment, I hear You calling me out of my world of cares. They are on the left and on the right; they're everywhere I'm looking. Lord, help me to focus on the things of the Spirit, to be Spirit-minded and not be entangled in the cares of this world. Forgive me for not trusting You with the affairs of my life. Right now, I give all of it to You! You are faithful! You are near to me! Your throne endures forever and that's where I want to dwell. Take it all, Lord! I come to You. You say You will give me rest. I receive it with thanksgiving. I run to Your throne. I know You will not reject me! You are my Refuge. Amen.

3

Signs

IN THE SPIRIT

I was driving a fancy sports car that had been given to me as a gift. I was trying to be very careful with it, as I was not used to driving such a nice car. I parked it at a curb next to some trees that had lost all their leaves to the fall winds. The ground was covered with leaves in shades of gold and red.

I hopped out of the car and jumped with childlike abandon in the leaves. They felt springy like a trampoline and I was enjoying myself. When I turned around, I noticed my sports car was gone. I started screaming, "Where is my car? Give me my car back!" A man standing nearby informed me my car had been impounded.

As quickly as I could, I found and went inside the warehouse where impounded cars were held. I told the people there, "Give me my car back!" Two men told me that I couldn't park next to the curb where I had left my car. "I didn't see the warning," I shouted at them.

They were firm. "The sign there says, 'No parking; all cars will be impounded,'" they told me. Again, I insisted I hadn't seen the sign.

Another told me I was not even supposed to be in the very building in which I was now standing! "Didn't you see the sign that said, 'Do Not Enter?'" he asked me.

I argued that I could not see the signs, that they weren't in plain view. I hadn't seen a single sign, yet they continued to insist the warnings had been there all along.

· · · · ·

IN THE WORD

Galatians 6:4-5, TPT
Let everyone be devoted to fulfill the work God has given them to do with excellence, and their joy will be in doing what's right and being themselves, and not in being affirmed by others. Every believer is ultimately responsible for his or her own conscience.

Exodus 4:8, NLT

The Lord said to Moses, "If they do not believe you and are not convinced by the first miraculous sign, they will be convinced by the second sign."

Ezekiel 3:17, NKJV

Son of man; I have made you a watchman to the house of Israel: therefore hear the word at my mouth; and give them warning from me.

1 Timothy 4:14, TPT

Do not neglect the spiritual gift you received through the prophecy spoken over you when the elders of the church laid their hands on you.

James 1:17, TPT

Every gift God freely gives us is good and perfect, streaming down from the Father of lights, who shines from the heavens with no hidden shadow or darkness and is never subject to change.

PRAYER

Lord, I've done it again. I have slacked off and played around, shrugging off my responsibility of using the gifts You have given me to bring glory to You. Forgive me for any passivity or neglect on my part. I am sorry for running off to what selfishly looks "fun," and tossing Your gifts to the side.

I will pay attention to Your signs, speaking to me clearly to respond to the call of the Spirit. I am sorry for "parking" my gift by the wayside. By Your grace and Spirit, I ask for a greater impartation of the gifts and commit myself to watching the signs and being faithful to You. I want to bless You! Your Word says that You never take the gifts away, and that's amazing. Thank You for the gifts; please grant me more as I walk in obedience to You. Amen.

4

Cutting Horse

IN THE SPIRIT

I was mingling with a crowd of people in the center of a rodeo arena. There was a rush of wind from the left side as a man, whom I knew was Jesus, came riding a large buckskin horse. He was heading towards me at full speed.

The other people ran to the fence of the arena while I stood watching, and then quickly tried to run to the right. The horse planted his feet in the dirt and took a stance in front of me, ready to move in a split second, like a cutting horse. He was trying to cut me out and separate me from the crowd. (Note: A cutting horse is a stock horse, typically an American Quarter Horse, bred and trained for "cutting," an equestrian competition requiring a horse and rider to separate a single cow from a herd of cattle and prevent it from getting back to the herd.)

Every time I took my focus off the Lord, the horse would appear in front of me, heading off my actions and thoughts. No matter if I turned to the left or the right, there He was, right there. There was no way could I take my focus off of Him, as He was drawing my attention to Him at each moment. This continued until we were in a face-to-face, head-to-head meeting, where He began to speak to me about the secrets of my heart.

· · · · ·

IN THE WORD

2 Timothy 2:8, TPT
But make Jesus, the Anointed One, your focus in life and ministry. For he came to earth as the descendant of David and rose from the dead, according to the revelation of the gospel that God has given me.

Numbers 16:21, KJV
Separate yourselves from among this congregation . . .

Proverbs 4:27, TPT
Do not turn to the right or the left; remove your foot from evil.

Isaiah 30:21, NKJV

Your ears shall hear a word behind you, saying, "This is the way, walk in it," whenever you turn to the right hand or whenever you turn to the left.

Luke 15:20, TPT

So the young son set off for home. From a long distance away, his father saw him coming, dressed as a beggar, and great compassion swelled up in his heart for his some who was returning home. So the father raced out to meet him . . .

Philippians 4:8, TPT

So keep your thoughts continually fixed on all that is authentic and real, honorable and admirable, beautiful and respectful, pure and holy, merciful and kind. And fasten your thoughts on every glorious work of God, praising him always.

3 John 1:14, NLT

For I hope to see you soon, and then we will talk face to face.

PRAYER

It takes time and practice, Lord, to separate myself from the crowds of this world and give myself fully to You. You pursue me with gusto! How can I ever thank You enough for chasing me down every time I wander in my thoughts? To focus on You and Your goodness is the only true value in this game called life. Forgive me, Lord, for looking to the left and the right, for trying to mix and mingle with the crowd, for not desiring the pleasure of meeting with You face to face more often. Once again, call me, chase me down, draw me to You. I will put a demand on my life to seek You out. By Your grace, I can do it and be consistent in it. Thank you, Lord, for heading me off at the pass and saving me. Amen.

5

The Classroom

IN THE SPIRIT

I saw a scene of a college classroom, in which a professor was writing physics formulas on a green chalkboard. These formulas told the story of how things work. (Physics is the science or set of laws that deal with matter, energy, and the way they act on each other in heat, light, electricity, and sound.)

The professor continued writing as a student went forward and erased a spot in the middle of the equations on the board. He took a piece of chalk and simply wrote: 1+1=2, turned around to the class, and said, "It is finished!" I sensed that the long formulas represented the long list of laws, rules, and regulations that religion spells out for us to live by, even to be saved. The simple equation the student wrote on the board is this: 1 is God's grace, +1 is faith, = 2 is salvation—the simplicity of the gospel!

IN THE WORD

Psalm 51:12, NLT

Restore to me the joy of your salvation, and make me willing to obey you.

Romans 3:31, NKJV

Do we then make void the law through faith? Certainly not! On the contrary, we establish the law.

Romans 10:4, NKJV

For Christ is the end of the law for righteousness to everyone who believes.

Romans 10:9-10, NLT

If you openly declare that Jesus is Lord and believe in your heart that God raised him from the dead, you will be saved. For it is by believing in your heart that you are made right with God, and it is by openly declaring your faith that you are saved.

1 Corinthians 2:1-2, MSG

You'll remember, friends, that when I first came to you to let you in on God's master stroke, I didn't try to impress you with polished speeches and the latest philosophy. I deliberately kept it plain and simple: first Jesus and who He is; then Jesus and what He did—Jesus crucified.

Ephesians 2:8, KJV

By grace you are saved, through faith, not of yourselves, it is a gift from God.

· · · · ·

PRAYER

Yes, Lord, it's as simple as that: to believe in my heart that Jesus is the Son of God, that He was crucified, died, was buried, and was raised from the dead and now sits at the right hand of the Father. This He did to save me, which is to make me whole in my spirit, soul, and body. I ask You to forgive my sins and wash me clean. Come into me, Lord, and be my Lord. Be the King of my life. I don't need complicated religion. I need a true relationship with You. I receive Your forgiveness. I will choose Your life. I will follow after the things of Your Spirit. Fill me to overflowing like I've never experienced before. Revive me, Lord. Give me the joy of Your salvation. Thank You. Amen.

6

Crawlspace

IN THE SPIRIT

I saw an old house that stood on a concrete foundation. The entrance to the crawlspace under the house was open. Its two doors, which were made of iron bars, had been taken off of the opening and set to the side.

Inside the crawlspace it was dark, except for the glowing, piercing yellow eyes that peered out of it. My sense in this picture was that this crawlspace was a place well known to the owner of the house, full of familiar choices, ideas, and memories. It was as if it had a life of its own, wooing the owner of the house to come into its recesses, into that familiar place of darkness and sins from the past.

There was also a sense that this opening represented a choice of whether to lock the doors and never return, or go back in and be once again entangled with the dark foundations of the past.

IN THE WORD

Joshua 24:15, KJV

And if it seems evil to you to serve the Lord, choose for yourselves this day whom you will serve . . . But as for me and my house, we will serve the Lord.

Nahum 1:15, MSG

Look! Striding across the mountains-a messenger bringing the latest good news: peace! A holiday, Judah! Celebrate! Worship and recommit to God! No more worries about this enemy. This one is history. Close the books.

John 8:34-36, NLT

Jesus replied, "I tell you the truth, everyone who sins is a slave of sin. A slave is not a permanent member of the family, but a son is part of the family forever. So if the Son sets you free, you are truly free."

Acts 12:10-11, MSG

Past the first guard and then the second, they came to the iron gate that led into the city, It swung open before them on it's own, and they were out on the street, free as the breeze. . . . Peter realized it was no dream. "I can't believe it—this really happened!"

Galatians 5:1, TPT

Let me be clear, the Anointed One has set us free-not partially, but completely and wonderfully free! We must always cherish this truth and stubbornly refuse to go back into the bondage of our past.

Hebrews 1:10, NKJV

You, Lord, in the beginning laid the foundation of the earth, And the heavens are the work of Your hands.

. . . . . .

PRAYER

As for me and my house, we will serve You, Lord. You have set us free from the sin and bondages hidden in our past. Choices we made led us into darkness. Forgive us, Lord, for being attracted once again to those wooing sins and voices. Thank You that You have set us free.

Indeed! You have laid a foundation of greatness and victory. We choose today to walk in Your goodness. We close the gates to the past. We lock the doors with the powerful name of Jesus and the power of the Spirit. Today we recommit to You in thanksgiving and surrender. It's a day of celebration and worship, for there are no more worries about our enemies. Praise the Lord! Amen.

7

Oyster Bed

IN THE SPIRIT

I was walking along a seashore. Scattered along it were many white oysters with their shells split wide open. Inside each one was a luminous and magnificent white pearl.

I saw the Lord walking up the rocky beach towards the pearls. Suddenly, He turned around, as if He'd been called by someone. Facing away from the oysters and pearls, He knelt down on one knee and scooped up an oyster that was different than all the others, one with a dark-colored shell. Inside that shell was a black pearl. He held it up to His chest, and coddled it as if it were something precious to Him.

IN THE WORD

Psalm 49:8, TPT
For redemption of their soul is precious . . .

Psalm 72:12-14, NLT
He will rescue the poor when they cry to Him; He will help the oppressed, who have no one to defend them. He feels pity for the weak and the needy, and He will rescue them. He will redeem them from oppression and violence, for their lives are precious to Him.

Psalm 139:17-18, TPT
Every single moment You are thinking of me! How precious and wonderful to consider that You cherish me constantly in Your every thought! O God, Your desires toward me are more than the grains of sand on every shore!

Matthew 18:12-13, TPT
Think of it this way: if a man owns a hundred sheep and one lamb wanders away and is lost, won't he leave the ninety-nine grazing and go out and thoroughly search for the one lost lamb? And if he finds his lost lamb, he rejoices over it, more than over the ninety-nine who are safe.

Romans 8:14-15, NKJV

For as many as are led by the Spirit of God, they are the sons of God. For you have not received the spirit of bondage again to fear; but you have received the Spirit of adoption, whereby we cry, Abba, Father.

. . . . .

PRAYER

Lord, You have called me out! You know my name! How joyous I am that You have not forgotten me in my isolation, rebellion, and shame. Forgive me for those attitudes. You are precious to me; how can I thank You?

I choose now to come to You in the same way You have come to me. You are vulnerable, so I make myself vulnerable to You. You leave the many to find the few and I am so blessed by Your compassion. Lord, use me, make me an instrument, fine-tuned in Your hands. Help me to hold others as dearly as You hold me. Bless me dear God, with Your unfailing love. Amen.

8

Ah-Ha Moment

IN THE SPIRIT

Before me were some people in a house, gathered at a screen door that opened to a lush backyard. They were struggling to get a clear picture of the view before them. All they saw was a dim view, distorted by the screen. One of them opened the door and there was an audible gasp from all of them—an "ah-ha" moment, as they could all now clearly see the view.

In the group, there was a man whose eyes were dim and he could not see to read. He put on a pair of prescription glasses, and found he could all of a sudden read the words on a printed page. It was another "ah-ha" moment, as he could now read everything clearly.

I sensed they represented many who look at the world and the Kingdom of God as if they were looking through a screen door. Their view is hindered, distorted, shaded, and dim. But by the grace of God, when there is a hungry heart for the things of the Lord, the door is opened and all is clear, bright, and full of life!

In the same way, a dimly sighted man puts on prescription glasses for the first time and sees, really sees, the Truth in front of him—how exciting!

· · · · · ·

IN THE WORD

Proverbs 14:16, MSG
Cynics look high and low for wisdom—and never find it; the open minded find it right on their doorstep!

1 Corinthians 13:2, MSG
. . . we don't see things clearly, we're squinting in a fog, peering through a mist. But, it won't be long before the weather clears and the sun shines bright. We'll see it all clearly then, see it all as clearly as God sees us, knowing Him directly, just as He knows us.

Isaiah 32:3, KJV
. . . and the eyes of them that see will not be dim, and the ears of them that hear will hearken.

Matthew 13:13, NLT

Therefore speak I to them in parables: because they, seeing, see not; and hearing they hear not, neither do they understand.

Ephesians 1:18, NLT

I pray that your hearts will be flooded with light so that you can understand the confident hope he has given to those he called—his holy people who are his rich and glorious inheritance.

. . . . .

PRAYER

Lord, Holy Spirit, take away any dimness or shortsightedness from me. Open my eyes to see through an opened door into Your heart and into the heavenlies. I want to see You, to know You, to pursue You with clarity.

Open my eyes, Lord! Take away all dimness. Give me a heart of strength to chase after You and not grow weary. Remove all barriers to my spiritual sight. Unstick me from my past perceptions. Awaken new sight, new vision. I need to know Your heart of love towards me and others. Again, open my eyes Lord! Amen.

MORE MUSINGS

9

Woodstock

IN THE SPIRIT

I watched a river before me, flowing from the right to the left, and noticed that, in the water, there were people! I saw the heads of joyous swimmers bobbing along in a group, all laughing and smiling. Following along behind them was an empty wooden boat. Some people were getting out of the river and scampering up the rock banks to a dry, grassy field above. They didn't look back.

There were about a hundred people in the river and just as many leaving. To the far right of where I stood, behind the boat, were the "headwaters" of the river. There, I could see more people, hurrying to get into the water. Most of them started by dipping their toes in, and then ran into the river, deeper and deeper. It reminded me of a movie I had seen, about how people came to the Woodstock music festival in 1969. They were more than enthusiastic and came in droves!

One lady in my vision, who was very excited to get near the water, was dipping her toes in, laughing and lifting up the front of her dress in a dance, exposing a pair of old-fashioned bloomers.

I had this impression: *"There is a time to come, or is upon us now, where there will be a joining of the various bodies of churches. The combined churches will flow with greater anointing and power. There will be some that don't agree with the newness of it, and fall away into dry places, but those that stay will be full of joy and the power of agreement. There is a place of rest and peace in the midst of all the newness. Those that find it will rise above any adversity and float on by it. This newness will attract many; as like Woodstock, it will call people from across the land. The addition of more mature people (represented by the woman with the old-fashioned bloomers), with skills and abilities, will add strength in the days ahead as the flow of the river branches out into more and bigger rivers."*

IN THE WORD

Ezekiel 47:2-5, KJV

Then brought he me out of the way of the gate northward, and led me about the way without unto the utter gate by the way the looketh eastward, and behold, there ran out waters on the right side. And when the man that had the line in his hand went forth eastward, he measured a thousand cubits, and he brought me through the waters; the waters were to the ankles. Again he measured a thousand, and brought me through the waters; the waters were to the knees. Again he measured a thousand, and brought me through; the waters were to the loins. Afterward he measured a thousand; and it was a river that I could not pass over: for the waters were risen, waters to swim in, a river that could not be passed over.

2 Thessalonians 2:3, KJV

Let no man deceive you, for that day will not come, except first comes a falling away, and that man of sin be revealed, the son of perdition.

Isaiah 55:1, KJV

Ho, everyone that thirsteth, come ye to the waters, and he that hath no money; come ye, buy and eat; yea, come, buy wine and mild without money and without price.

Psalm 16:11, KJV

For thou wilt shew me the path of life: in thy presence is fullness of joy; at Thy right hand there are pleasures forever more.

· · · · ·

PRAYER

Ho, I thirst for You God! Running to Your fullness, I can't seem to get enough. Take me deeper into Your presence—not just to my ankles, but all the way in. I want to be in over my head! Let all those who seek You come! Come many, come thirsty, come to the waters. In Your presence, Lord, we find our peace and joy. Thank You for Your goodness towards us. Call in those who will add to the Kingdom. Add confidence, giftings, and competence. We long to be with You. Take us deeper. Join our hearts like never before. But then, dear God, send us out. Give us the grace to be world changers for You. Amen.

10

Valley of Decision

IN THE SPIRIT

I saw Jesus standing on a hill overlooking a great and expansive valley. Below Him were dozens upon dozens of sheep fleeces strewn across the green valley floor.

I sensed that these fleeces had intentionally been placed there. Some would receive the dew from heaven, others would not—like Gideon's fleece in Judges 6, where Gideon trusted God to help him make a decision by whether a sheep fleece left out overnight was wet or dry in the morning. It was as if the fleeces I saw in my vision represented many decisions that needed to be made—spiritual decisions, on which people's fate for eternity hung in the balance—but these were being left to chance.

I felt Jesus was overseeing these situations with longing heart, not wanting anyone to leave their eternal destiny to chance.

IN THE WORD

Judges 6:37, NLT
Prove it to me in this way. I will put a wool fleece on the threshing floor tonight, if the fleece is wet with dew in the morning but the ground is dry, then I will know that you are going to help me rescue Israel as you promised.

2 Peter 3:9, TPT
This means that, contrary to man's perspective, the Lord is not late with his promise to return, as some measure lateness. But rather, his "delay" simply reveals his loving patience toward you, because he does not want any to perish but all to come to repentance.

Malachi 3:10, NLT
"Bring all the tithes, the tenth into the storehouse, so there may be food in my house, and test me now in this," says the Lord of hosts. "If I will not open for you the windows of heaven and pour out for you so great a blessing until there is no more room to receive it."

Psalms 119:66, TPT
Teach me how to make good decisions, and give me revelation-light, for I believe in your commands.

Isaiah 30:21, NLT

Your own ears will hear him. Right behind you a voice will say, "This is the way you should go," whether to the right or to the left.

· · · · ·

PRAYER

Dear God, there lies before me a multitude of decisions I don't feel qualified to make. I lay out fleeces, hoping You will answer me this way. Will they be graced with morning dew? What should I do? I am in an agonizing situation without Your guidance. Show me, teach me how to make good decisions. Give me revelation, for I believe in Your commands. Forgive me for stepping out without You. It never goes right that way. You have the power to rescue me from my own perspective. I will trust in Your timing from here on out. I will commit myself to being faithful, knowing that You will pour out Your wisdom and blessings on me. I wait! Amen.

YOUR MUSINGS

11

Dam

IN THE SPIRIT

I saw a dam standing in the midst of a river. It was as tall as the Grand Coulee Dam (which is located in my home state of Washington). This dam in my vision had clearly not been built in one pour of concrete, nor in one single day. It was made up of sections that had been placed on top of one another.

A figure of a man stood on the top of the dam, overlooking the valley below. There was a large reservoir of water behind Him that was as vast as the sea. The water was dotted with white-capped waves. I could see that the reservoir was full, but the water could not go over the dam.

Below, in the valley, was a dry riverbed. I could see people—dozens and dozens, maybe hundreds of them—laying on it, on the dry ground, with their heads facing in the direction of the dam. The word "Desperate" was written on the pant leg of one of the people. The figures were all silent and still.

Every now and then, the Man on the dam would wave His left arm to the side, as if calling for something. A wind would blow through each time He beckoned. When He did this, a floodgate would open up and water gushed forth over the side of the dam. The water dried on the hot concrete as it flowed downward.

At times, a few sprays of water showered the valley below, but not enough to moisturize it. The Man repeated the wave of His arm many times, with the same results. As He waved, He shouted, "Rise up; you must make an effort towards Me, come!" But nothing changed.

· · · · ·

IN THE WORD

Psalm 85:7, TPT
Pour out even more of your love on us! Reveal more of your kindness and restore us back to you.

Psalm 89:9, TPT
You rule over oceans and the swelling seas. When their stormy waves rise, you speak, and they lie still.

Psalm 104:30, TPT

When you release your Spirit-wind, life is created, ready to replenish life upon the earth.

Psalm 142:6, TPT

Please listen to my heart's cry, for I am low and in desperate need of you!

Ezekiel 47:9, NLT

There will be swarms of living things wherever the water of this river flows. Fish will abound in the Dead Sea, for its waters will become fresh. Life will flourish wherever this water flows.

Matthew 8:27, NLT

The disciples were amazed. "Who is this man?" they asked. "Even the winds and waves obey him!"

Hebrews 1:1, TPT

. . . The revelation he gave them was only a fragment at a time, building one truth upon another.

Revelation 7:16, NKJV

Their souls will be completely satisfied. And neither the sun nor any scorching heat will affect them.

Revelation 22:17, NKJV

And the Spirit and the bride say, "Come!" And let him who thirsts come. Whoever desires, let him take the water of life freely.

PRAYER

How can You be so gracious to us? You watch over us and pour out Your Spirit on us, yet we falter when it comes to receiving You.

We admit we are desperate; we turn our faces in Your direction, Creator and Ruler of the wind and seas. As You call to us, give us ears to hear You, and hearts to be obedient to Your call to Come. The barrier between us was not formed by one event, but in many frustrations, sins, and sometimes just plain procrastination. Forgive us, Lord!

As You release Your Spirit on us once again, give us strength and boldness to rise up and take hold of what You are offering. We are not desperate, not in light of Your care and the power of Your Spirit. Lord, reveal more of Your love and kindness as You restore us to Yourself. We call out for Your Spirit. Let Your river flow over us and cause us to truly live the life only You can give. We rise up! Amen.

IT'S NOT *time* FOR A BREAK.

12

Vineyard

IN THE SPIRIT

Acres and acres of vineyards covered a rolling hillside with beautiful green vines, leaves, and ripe fruit. As I soaked in this beautiful sight before me, I heard, "There's a time to sow and a time to reap, a time to build and a time to heal."

At this, droves of people poured into the vineyard. There were those equipped with pruning shears, shovels, fertilizer, and insecticide. They were all working at their project of tending to the vineyard. As they worked, I could feel the strong presence of the Vinekeeper and I knew the King was among them.

A strong word came upon me saying, "It's not time for a break." The people, apparently hearing it too, continued to tend to the vines.

IN THE WORD

Ecclesiastes 3:1-3, NLT
For everything there is a season, a time for every activity under heaven. A time to be born and a time to die. A time to plant and a time to harvest. A time to kill and a time to heal. A time to tear down and a time to build up.

Song of Songs 2:15, NLT
Catch all the foxes, those little foxes, before they ruin the vineyard of love, for the grapevines are blossoming!

Jeremiah 31:3-5, NLT
Long ago the Lord said to Israel: I have loved you, my people, with an everlasting love. With unfailing love I have drawn you to myself. I will rebuild you, my virgin Israel. You will again be happy and dance merrily with your tambourines. Again you will plant your vineyards on the mountains of Samaria and eat from your own gardens there.

Haggai 2:4, NLT
"Be strong, all you people still left in the land. And now get to work, for I am with you," says the Lord of Heaven's Armies.

2 Thessalonians 3:13, NKJV
But as for you, brethren, do not grow weary in doing good.

Matthew 11:28, MSG

"Are you tired? Worn out? Burned out on religion? Come to me. Get away with me and you'll recover your life. I'll show you how to take a real rest. Walk with me and work with me-watch how I do it. Learn the unforced rhythms of grace. I won't lay anything heavy or ill-fitting on you. Keep company with me and you'll learn to live freely and lightly."

1 Corinthians 7:20, NKJV

Let every man abide in the same calling wherein he was called.

. . . . . .

PRAYER

Lord, sometimes I see so much to do for the Kingdom. Show me my part, my gifts, purpose, and calling. I give You my all. Just show me the areas where You want me to invest my time and energy. This is the season to be about my Father's business. I ask for Your strength to help me in tending to Your vineyard. I see the planting and reaping, and I see the building and healing. It's all about You! You are in our midst. You never leave us alone. Thank You for calling me to this work. I will take great pleasure in serving and pleasing You alongside my brothers and sisters. I won't grow weary; You are my strength. I will walk with You and learn the unforced rhythms of grace. Bless You, King among us! Amen.

YOUR MUSINGS

13

Passage

IN THE SPIRIT

In my dream, I saw myself hanging out a hotel window near a park. I saw a bridge to my left and a water passage straight in front of me. A repair man was running from the right hollering, "We are not allowing the tide to come in. The passage is being drained for repair!"

As the waters receded, the "riverbed" became dry, with patches and puddles of water and mud. People from the shore began to enter the riverbed and walk in the dry places. The number of people increased as they saw the dry ground.

The people then began to bring their garbage and dump it in the riverbed. There was garden waste, plastic bags full of garbage, a huge pile of electronics—computers, cell phones, and other devices. Along the banks, people were dumping old appliances, more garbage, and yard waste.

The riverbed was now steaming and had a gross stench. Then, in a moment, without warning, the tide waters were released. The people ran to the shore and the garbage floated and moved along with the flow of the tide. I heard, "Garbage in, garbage out."

· · · · ·

IN THE WORD

Isaiah19:5, NKJV
And the waters shall fail from the sea, and the rivers will be wasted and dried up.

Isaiah 58:12, NKJV
Those from among you shall build the old waste places; you shall raise up the foundations of many generations, and you shall be called the Repairer of the Breach, the Restorer of Streets to Dwell In.

Acts 3:19, KJV
Repent ye therefore and be converted that your sins may be blotted out, when the times of refreshing will come from the presence of the Lord.

1 Corinthians 3:16, NKJV

Do you not know that you are the temple of God and that the Spirit of God dwells in you?

Ephesians 5:26, KJV

. . . that He might sanctify and cleanse it with the washing of water by the word.

Philippians 3:8, NLT

Yes, everything else is worthless when compared with the infinite value of knowing Christ Jesus my Lord. For His sake I have discarded everything else, counting it as garbage, so that I could gain Christ.

2 Timothy 2:21, KJV

If any man purge himself from these, he shall be a vessel of honor, sanctified and ready for the master's use and prepared for every good work.

. . . . .

PRAYER

Thank You, God! You have given me the grace to—once again, by Your Spirit—clean this temple of the garbage in my life.

Though it seems like a lifetime, Your purging process can happen in a blink of the eye. Forgive me, Lord, for hanging onto old habit patterns, thoughts, bitterness, and things that are just pure garbage when it compares to Your holiness. Wash me as I yield to Your Spirit in this temple.

I long to know, to gain, Christ. Sanctify me and cleanse me with the washing of Your word. I can see it! I see the restoration and refreshing that comes from Your presence. So come, Lord! Let my awareness of Your presence be enhanced. Release Your waters and cleanse this temple! Amen.

14

Birthday

IN THE SPIRIT

I walked into a large house that appeared empty. As I explored it, I came upon a room with a woman on a bed. She was partially sitting up, and looked at me as I stood in the doorway. At the same time, a group of people walked up behind me and peered over my shoulder into the room, looking at her. They left suddenly, and I walked inside the room.

The woman was in labor and was making little progress in the delivery. I asked if she had help for the birth. She answered, "No, I am all alone." The other people would come by now and then and peer into the room, but no one offered assistance. I decided to stay and help.

Shortly, I told her it was time to push the baby out. She sighed and lay down, saying weakly, " I can't; I don't have the strength." She was uncomfortable, but not in pain. She couldn't push, but I could see the baby needed to come out. I examined her and the baby. As I was doing this, the peering people came by and said I should not be doing that. They said, "You are reaching too far!" The woman told them she wanted my help and they fell quiet.

I noticed that the baby was not in a good position for delivery. I was able to re-position him so he could be safely delivered. When he was safely out, I presented him to his joyful mother. All the other people left. Oddly, there was no clean up. I, too, left the woman with her baby, alone.

I sensed these words impressed on me: *"The time is upon us; the time is at hand when those who have been called to the delivery must show themselves ready. The Lord has prepared His place and His time for the people called by His name, to bring forth what is ready to be delivered into this time. There is comfort and there is joy and there is sometimes weeping, but God's hand is not too short that it cannot save. It's not time to be an onlooker. It's not your call to simply peer in at the delivery of such a great thing the Lord is doing in this time.*

"You who are simply onlookers will not be partakers of the glory or the joy and comfort. It's a hands-on experience I am calling you to! This is the moment and this is the time. I have readied my people. I have readied my delivery place. I call forth; I shout to my people: 'Ready, ready, ready yourselves and be ready, always ready. Hear Me, the hands of my servants must toil for this delivery of my glory, comfort and joy.'"

IN THE WORD

Isaiah 37:3, NKJV
This day is a day of trouble and rebuke and blasphemy; for the children have come to birth, but there is no strength to bring them forth.

Isaiah 59:1, KJV
Behold, the Lord's hand is not shortened, that it cannot save; nor His ear heavy, that it cannot hear.

Isaiah 66:7, NKJV
Before she was in labor, she gave birth. Before her pain came, she delivered a male child. Who has heard such a thing? Who has seen such things? Shall the earth be made to give birth in one day? Or shall a nation be born at once? For as soon as Zion was in labor, She gave birth to her children. Shall I bring to the time of birth, and not cause delivery?" says the Lord. "Shall I who cause delivery shut up the womb?" says your God.

1 Timothy 2:1, NKJV
Therefore I exhort first of all that supplications, prayers, intercessions, and giving of thanks be made for all men . . .

Hebrews 3:14, NKJV
For we have become partakers of Christ if we hold the beginning of our confidence steadfast to the end,

PRAYER

Open our eyes, Lord, to see Your timing and Your plans. We recognize You calling us to move in intercession at this time that You call "ready." Forgive us, Lord, for not giving our all, for only peering in on the delivery of such great things as You would bring forth. Our personal houses of prayer have grown silent and we have not prayed through the veil of Your plan.

Give us the breath of prayer. Keep us in Your care as You are bringing to the fullness a time that is ready. We need Your strength to bring it forth. We ask You for the skill, the persistence, and the true readiness to be a part of the great things You have placed before us. We don't want to be onlookers only peering in on Your works. We want to be partakers of Your joy, comfort, and glory.

Ready us, Lord! Give us great boldness to move ahead with You. We call for Your mercy and grace. Bless us, Lord, with the power of prayer so we can see Your glory. Show us Your glory, Lord! Amen.

YOUR MUSINGS

15

Apartment

IN THE SPIRIT

In this dream, I was living in a small apartment—a high rise in a big city. It had one very tall and skinny rectangular window, looking out over the city, and one door.

My landlord came to me and told me I had to move, and to choose another room in the building. I was given three choices: a room with no windows, a room with three windows, or a room with wall-to-wall, floor-to-ceiling windows on three sides and a door on the other. I chose the latter. It had a beautiful garden view, and when my back was facing the door, I looked out upon a beautiful backdrop of rhododendrons in full bloom with red flowers. I could see no further beyond them.

The landlord began hinting that I needed to pay rent. Of course, I couldn't live there for free! I told him, "I will give you something soon, as soon as I see what is in my heart to do." In my dream, I was moving in some knick-knacks and putting them on the window sills when I suddenly woke up.

As I reflected and prayed about this dream, I realized it spoke of moving from one place of "seeing" prophetically from the perspective of only a small window with a limited view, to a new, larger place of greater vision. It spoke to moving to God's greater perspective, and no longer looking at things behind nor too far into the future.

I believe the rent for the landlord represented that this place will have a "cost," although it may not be a literal one. There will be a price that must be paid (sacrifice). Putting away the knick-knacks tells me that the moving in has already begun.

......

IN THE WORD

1 Samuel 9:9, NLT
(In those days, if people wanted a message from God, they would say, "Let's go and ask the seer," for prophets used to be called seers.)

2 Samuel, 24:24, NLT

But the king replied to Araunah, "No, I insist on buying it, for I will not present burnt offerings to the Lord my God that have cost me nothing..."

Song of Songs 2:1, TPT

I am truly his rose, the very theme of his song. I'm overshadowed by his love, growing in the valley!

Isaiah 54:2, NLT

Enlarge your house; build an addition. Spread out your home and spare no expense!

Jeremiah 1:11-12, NLT

Then the Lord said to me, "Look, Jeremiah! What do you see?" And I replied, "I see a branch from an almond tree." And the Lord said, "That's right, and it means that I am watching and I will certainly carry out all my plans."

Matthew 13:11, TPT

... you've been given the intimate experience of insight into the hidden truths and mysteries of the realm of heaven's kingdom...

PRAYER

Dear Lord,

I want it all! I want to see more, to know more, and to have Heaven's perspective. I long for insight into hidden truths and mysteries of the realm of the Kingdom. I want to know the Father's heart and see what the Father sees. Move me on, Lord, to a place of insight that is far more expansive than what I experience right now. I choose to pay the price, whatever You say it costs, for this anointing and gifting from You. Thank You for the opportunity to grow in my calling. I recognize it's all about You! I look forward to a room with a view—a Kingdom view. Teach me how to see in this new way, to use my gifts to advance the Kingdom. Raise up the seers, Lord! Amen.

16

Duck

IN THE SPIRIT

On the floor before me lay many brightly colored pieces of a child's puzzle. The pieces were scattered and piled this way and that—very disorganized and disorderly. I tried to be creative and bring some order and design to the pieces. As I arranged the pieces my way, it looked perfect to me. It was the design of a colorful duck.

I sensed the Lord wanting to rearrange the pieces to create a perfect design, His way. He took the pieces and made the image of a house. It looked nothing like my duck at all.

I heard: "Like pieces of a child's puzzle, your image of the way your life should look has been designed by you. You built it your way. It looks perfect and normal to you, but it's only a duck."

Perfection for your life is only in God's design. The pieces of your life must be made into the image of His choice. His design looks nothing at all like a duck. It is more the design of a "house of prayer."

IN THE WORD

Proverbs 19:21, TPT
A person may have many ideas concerning God's plan for his life, but only the designs of his purpose will succeed in the end.

Ecclesiastes 3:11, NLT
Yet God has made everything beautiful for its own time. He has planted eternity in the human heart, but even so, people cannot see the whole scope of God's work from beginning to end.

Ephesians 5:27, TPT
All that he does in us is designed to make us a mature church for his pleasure, until we become a source of praise to him-glorious and radiant, beautiful and holy, without fault or flaw.

Jeremiah 10:14, NLT
The whole human race is foolish and has no knowledge! The craftsmen are disgraced by the idols they make, for their carefully shaped works are a fraud. These idols have no breath or power.

1 Corinthians 15:49, KJV
And as we have borne the image of the earthy, we shall also bear the image of the heavenly.

Proverbs 2:11, TPT

If you choose to follow good counsel, divine design will watch over you and understanding will protect you from making poor choices.

· · · · ·

PRAYER

I've done it again! Once more, I have succeeded in creating a life that bears the image of... an earthly life. In comparison to what You want to build my life into, my version looks like a misshapen duck. Really, a duck?! I have taken all the pieces and parts I think would look nice as my life, and fashioned them my way. Forgive me for taking over the designing project.

Lord, please rework the pieces of my life and make it beautiful in Your time. Make it into Your divine design. I want to see Your work in my life. My ideas just haven't worked out! I want my life to be full of praise to You, bearing Your image.

Mature me; make me a source of praise to You, glorious and radiant, beautiful and holy, without fault or flaw. I want to look like You, Lord. Make me a house of prayer. You are perfect in all Your ways. Bless the Lord, O my soul! Amen.

17

Fog

IN THE SPIRIT

With my spiritual eyes, I could see there was a dense fog lying over a congregation of people. It was the kind of fog that is lazy and thick, covering a low-lying valley. Along with the fog came a sense of physical, emotional, and spiritual dullness. My spirit felt dry as it experienced the all-encompassing fog.

In this dream, a true story came to my mind. It was about a group of patients in a Bronx, New York hospital who were being treated by a neurologist with an experimental drug for Parkinson's Disease. The degenerative affliction had left this group of people listless, lethargic, and mentally foggy. The amazing positive results of this experiment were listed as: mental clarity, physical mobility, and a new zest for life.

The timing of this story led me to believe that this was God's intention. The fog was to represent the spiritual dullness that was overtaking His people, and His love and Spirit were to awaken them and break through the fog.

·····

IN THE WORD

Isaiah 32:3, NKJV
The eyes of those who see will not be dim, And the ears of those who hear will listen.

Isaiah 60:12, NKJV
Arise, shine; for your light has come! And the glory of the Lord is risen upon you. For behold, the darkness shall cover the earth, and deep darkness the people; But the Lord will arise over you, And His glory will be seen upon you.

Ezekiel 37:6, NLT
I will put breath into you, and you will come to life. Then you will know that I am the Lord.

John 8:12, TPT
Then Jesus said, "I am light to the world and those who embrace me will experience life-giving light, and they will never walk in darkness."

Matthew 17:7, NLT

Then Jesus came over and touched them. "Get up," he said. "Don't be afraid."

Matthew 13:15, TPT

Their minds are dull and slow to perceive, their ears are plugged and are hard of hearing, and they have deliberately shut their eyes to the truth. Otherwise they would open their eyes to see, and open their minds to understand. Then they would turn to me and let me instantly heal them.

1 Corinthians 6:14, TPT

Now the God who raised up our Lord from the grave will awaken and raise us up through his mighty power!

. . . . .

PRAYER

Lord, help us! Your people are in a fog. It is lying dark over us and holding us back from seeing all that You are and all that we are in You. Holy Spirit, come and cleanse away the dross, take away the dullness, lift the fog. Take us to a higher place. Have we been caught in a disease of spiritual dullness? Blow through us now with the breath of Your Spirit. Bring us new life, new vigor, clarity, and zeal. Give us a spiritual remedy, as You are the Great Physician. Amen.

18

Shout

IN THE SPIRIT

I heard the age-old Christmas song ring out, "Do you hear what I hear?"

There was then a resounding reply from the heavenlies, "Do you hear what I hear?" This was followed by the sound of many foot soldiers marching in time. *Stomp, stomp, stomp,* was the sound they made, so loudly I felt the ground vibrate.

"Do you hear what I hear?" repeated the Voice. It continued: "I hear the sound of My people being ignited into readiness, breaking free from passivity and procrastination. I hear the sound of My people linking arms and marching to the same song. It's a song of battle, a song of Jericho. It's not the time to walk as though you are blinded to the times. It's time to move ahead with your voice, with your own trumpet. It's a time of waiting for the grand shout! Events of the days are calling to you to stir up the warrior within. Again I say, wait for the shout and move in the time of Jericho together. Sing a song of joy; your time is at hand!"

· · · · ·

IN THE WORD

Numbers 10:9, NLT
When you arrive in your own land and go to war against your enemies who attack you, sound the alarm with the trumpets.

Joshua 6:20, KJV
So the people shouted when the priests blew with the trumpets: and it came to pass, when the people heard the sound of the trumpet, and the people shouted with a great shout, that the wall fell down flat, so that the people went up into the city, every man straight before him and they took the city.

Psalm 47:5, NLT
God has ascended with a mighty shout. The Lord has ascended with trumpets blaring.

Mark 13:33, TPT

This is why you must be waiting, watching and praying, because no one knows when that season of time will come.

2 Timothy 2:3-4, TPT

Overcome every form of evil as a victorious soldier of Jesus the Anointed One. For every soldier called to active duty must divorce himself from the distractions of this world so that he may fully satisfy the One who chose him.

. . . . . .

PRAYER

We are thankful that You are the faithful God who hears. Without You, we are nothing and without one another our efforts are feeble. Unite us! Ignite us in readiness and unity, so we will no longer be slaves to passivity or procrastination. We march to the same song, which is a song of victory and a song of battle. The enemy will hear us coming. Give us the hearts of warriors! We shout the shouts of victory and our trumpets declare the battle is Yours, Lord! We wait on You, Lord. We wait for the Jericho battle cry. We won't move ahead of You for Your times are perfect. We are ready Lord; use us to advance the Kingdom. Amen.

YOUR MUSINGS

19

Ocean Liner

IN THE SPIRIT

The stormy waves of the deep ocean were high and white-capped; the wind was wicked and strong. There were many people in the water, who could barely stay afloat as they tried to tread the icy water. Before them, a dark blue and white ocean liner slowly sliced through the water as it moved beside them. They were forced to tread faster as the waters were troubled and dispersed by the vessel's immense presence. I heard the words, ". . . as two ships passing in the night." (This common expression generally refers to two people very briefly meeting each other, perhaps never to meet again.)

I knew there were many afflictions represented by the people in the ocean water. I could hear their cries for help and healing as the ship sailed by. "Help us," cried the people. "We are drowning! We are dying!"

Then I heard shouts from the people aboard the ship, saying, "Don't let the ship pass you by," and, "Don't miss the boat!"

Musing, I often find myself watching people with afflictions and ailments—people who need help—who *do* "miss the boat" or "let the ship pass them by." Oftentimes, it's a matter of engaging with the Healer, perhaps in special moments when He is present. There is no magic formula, but engagement with the Healer brings us into the Kingdom, where His perfection dwells.

· · · · ·

IN THE WORD

3 John 1:2, NLT
Dear friend, I hope all is well with you and that you are as healthy in body as you are strong in spirit.

Luke 5:17, NKJV
Now it happened on a certain day, as He was teaching, that there were Pharisees and teachers of the law sitting by, who had come out of every town of Galilee, Judea, and Jerusalem. And the power of the Lord was present to heal them.
(This word "present" is the Greek word eis, *which means "being into a thing." Interpreting this scripture, you could say that Jesus was "into" healing on that day).*

Exodus 33:19, NKJV

Then He said, "I will make all My goodness pass before you, and I will proclaim the name of the Lord before you. I will be gracious to whom I will be gracious, and I will have compassion on whom I will have compassion."

Psalm 34:19, NLT

The righteous person faces many troubles, but the Lord comes to the rescue each time.

· · · · ·

PRAYER

Lord, we cry out to the Lord, our Healer. Don't pass us by! Let Your healing flow! Draw us to You, Lord, so we can engage intimately with You. Call us out of the deep and stormy places. Healing is rightfully ours due to Your love, promises, and sacrifice. Victory is the anthem of the Cross.

In this moment, You are present to heal. I take hold of You—you are my Life Raft! I will not be unacquainted like a ship passing in the night. I will not miss the boat. Right now, I choose to take my healing. I am a possessor of divine health! Thank You forever! Yours is the Kingdom, the power, and the glory. Amen.

YOUR MUSINGS

20

Music

IN THE SPIRIT

The sky lit up with the color and depth of a brilliant blue neon sign. A white musical staff ran across the upper horizon as a treble clef floated into its proper place upon the staff. Another staff of music appeared below the first. A bass clef sign glowed on its lines. All clouds which were there naturally seemed to give way or become a part of the work the Lord was doing in the heavens. This image remained before me with almost overwhelming intensity. As I moved on, the vision faded slowly while the natural sky was still in formation and was a testimony to the reality of the vision.

As I reflected, I heard God saying, "Take a deep breath—lift up your hands, for in the skies above you I have opened the heavens and have painted the atmosphere with the vapor and fragrance of the music of my Spirit. The very music of heaven has hovered overhead. The sky has been filled with notes sung only on the heavenly treble clef, but this very hour, I am delivering to you passion found in the bass clef. Things of the deep are there and will soon be rightly available to you, My chosen, whose hearts hold the magnitude of my great love. More could hear, if more would prepare. I wait for you. Now, ask of Me and I will show you great and mighty things! I long for the cry of those who want more than just the fresh vapors of Heaven, for those who want and shall receive the mighty rains to saturate to their deepest being. I will flood this land with My goodness and glory so that all would know, surely, the God of Daniel, David, and many radical risk takers of this day. My glory does fill the whole earth!"

· · · · ·

IN THE WORD

Psalm 42:7, NKJV
Deep calls unto deep at the noise of Your waterfalls. All Your waves and billows have gone over me.

Psalm 92:5, NKJV
O Lord, how great are Your works! Your thoughts are very deep.

Psalm 96:1, KJV

Oh, sing to the Lord a new song! Sing to the Lord, all the earth.

Psalm 148:4, NLT

Praise him skies above! Praise him, vapors high above the clouds!

Isaiah 6:3, NKJV

And one cried to another and said: "Holy, holy, holy is the Lord of hosts; The whole earth is full of His glory."

Jeremiah 33:3, NKJV

Call to Me, and I will answer you, and show you great and mighty things, which you do not know.

· · · · ·

PRAYER

Lord, You show us Your marvelous works in the skies and all around us. Open our eyes to see You more in Your splendor. We want to hear Your heavenly songs. We want to have the heart of David, a heart that is after You. God, release the deep songs from Your heaven's bass clef. We want more; we want You. Amen.

21

Cloak

IN THE SPIRIT

I was walking through a forest—one that was made up of many different shades of vibrant green. I came to the edge of a cliff, overlooking a giant river gorge. On my back was a brown cloak, which I called a mantle. A voice said, "This is a representation of the gifts and anointing on your life. You can wear it, or you can take it off and choose not to wear it."

There were items attached to the mantle. Leaves and twigs had become stuck to it as I passed through the forest. There was a pin on the front, on one side of the chest, that reminded me of a pin one gets in the Air Force when given their "wings." The upper back was covered in porcupine quills and from the neckline of the cloak dangled two bear teeth.

Suddenly, I dropped the mantle and it floated down, slowly. With a clanging noise, it landed on a square plate of polished gold. As it hit, all of the items flew up and off the mantle, into the gorge below. The mantle was then plain, with nothing on it. I heard the words, "This is the True Mantle, one which is to be worn by My victorious saints. It is not to be altered or adulterated in any way. It is not to be adored nor adorned. This plain mantle is the garment of My true warriors and anointed ones whom I will exalt. This is the most honored garment , the mantle of Humility. Not everyone can wear it properly. Those who do have learned the lessons of the simplicity of its nature."

......

IN THE WORD

Exodus 28:36, NKJV
You shall also make a plate of pure gold and engrave on it, like the engraving of a signet: HOLINESS TO THE LORD.

Leviticus 20:7, NKJV
Consecrate yourselves therefore, and be holy, for I am the Lord your God.

Isaiah 3:18-22, NKJV

In that day the Lord will take away the finery: The jingling anklets, the scarves, and the crescents; The pendants, the bracelets, and the veils; The headdresses, the leg ornaments, and the headbands; The perfume boxes, the charms, and the rings; The nose jewels, the festal apparel, and the mantles...

Isaiah 10:27, KJV

And it shall come to pass in that day, that his burden shall be taken away from off thy shoulder, and his yoke from off thy neck, and the yoke shall be destroyed because of the anointing.

2 Kings 2:13, NKJV

He also took up the mantle of Elijah that had fallen from him, and went back and stood by the bank of the Jordan.

2 Timothy 2:3-4, 21, NKJV

You therefore must endure hardship as a good soldier of Jesus Christ. No one engaged in warfare entangles himself with the affairs of this life, that he may please him who enlisted him as a soldier. (vs.21) Therefore if anyone cleanses himself from the later, he will be a vessel for honor, sanctified and useful for the Master, prepared for every good work.

PRAYER

This is the day for allowing the Maker of the mantle to examine ours and purify them. We trust You, Lord, and lay them down for You. We ask for Your cleansing, refreshment, and healing before we walk under the cloak of Your anointing again. We, by the grace of God, will handle our anointings and gifts with the utmost honor and respect, to cherish them and do everything to be found approved in them. Lord, we all drop our mantles upon Your purity. We allow Your grace and mercy to cleanse us from the wounds and impurities that have influenced the use of the gifts that You have given us. We pray for Your forgiveness both for the known and unknown errors we have made in our walks as Your ambassadors. Forgive us for the misuse of our anointings and for any pride we may have been caught up in. Create in us pure hearts, God. Amen!

22

Honeycomb

IN THE SPIRIT

One day I saw Jesus mingling in a large crowd. He was walking among His people in all of His radiant glory. As He walked, He was handing out pieces of His own personal honeycomb. Each one of the people who received a chunk of the honeycomb was healed of one of many different sicknesses. And then, He came to you! He lifted up a piece of honeycomb that was the size of a car tire. He handed it to you, saying, "Eat this and be well! Give portions out to others for their health." You took the honeycomb and did as He said. All who ate the honeycomb were healed.

IN THE WORD

1 Samuel 14:27, NLT
. . . and he dipped the end of his stick into a piece of honeycomb and ate the honey. After he had eaten it, he felt refreshed.

Psalm 103:3, MSG
He forgives your sins—every one. He heals your diseases—every one.

Luke 9:1-2, TPT
Jesus summoned together his twelve apostles and imparted to them authority over every demon and the power to heal every disease. Then he commissioned them to preach God's kingdom realm and to heal the sick to demonstrate that the kingdom had arrived.

Proverbs 24:13, NLT
My child, eat honey, for it is good, and the honeycomb is sweet to the taste.

Jeremiah 33:6, NKJV
Behold, I will bring it health and healing; I will heal them and reveal to them the abundance of peace and truth.

Matthew 10:8, NLT

Heal the sick, raise the dead, cure those with leprosy, and cast out demons. Give as freely as you have received.

· · · · ·

PRAYER

Dear God, You have provided everything we need to live healthy and victorious lives here and now. Forgive us for not appropriating Your goodness. Right now, I receive what is rightfully mine, Your divine healing! I receive and partake of it—my portion of the honeycomb of Your goodness and faithfulness. Freely, You have given this healing and therefore, freely I receive it. Thank You, Lord, for giving me my portion. You forgive my sins; You heal my disease. I take the responsibility to deliver Your healing to others. You direct me to heal the sick, so may the sick be healed in Your name. Thank You, Lord! Amen.

23

IV Drip

IN THE SPIRIT

In a large auditorium, a great number of people were laying on hospital beds. They were weak and feeble, and dressed in thin hospital gowns. A nurse in a white uniform was administering an IV solution into each patient's arm. The people were weak without the solution, yet were only slightly revived by the IV drip.

I heard, "These people are on a 'drip feed' of my Spirit. It's my desire to give each My full flow. I long to open them up and pour out My abundance on them."

Some of the people said, "Yes, give it to me," while others were satisfied with the only the small droplets of relief. I sensed this signified that though some had had previous powerful encounters with the Lord— the "full flow"— they would benefit from a continual "drip feed" if they would receive it.

IN THE WORD

Isaiah 40:29, NLT
He gives power to the weak and strength to the powerless.

Job 26:2, NLT
How you have helped the powerless! How you have saved the weak!

Psalm 65:11, NKJV
You crown the year with Your goodness, And Your paths drip with abundance.

Psalm 68:3, NLT
But let the godly rejoice. Let them be glad in God's presence. Let them be filled with joy.

Psalm 85:6, TPT
Revive us again, O God! I know you will! Give us a fresh start! Then all your people will taste your joy and gladness.

1 Corinthians 2:12, NLT
And we have received God's Spirit (not the world's spirit), so we can know the wonderful things God has freely given us.

PRAYER

Help us, Lord! We become so weak and feeble sometimes, even in the things of the Spirit. We know You are the source of all power and goodness. We know You are our source for anything worthwhile. Forgive us for letting our fires burn low. Revive us, Lord! We ask for Your Spirit to rekindle, revive, and revisit us in our time of weakness. Pour out on us as we bow to You, the high and lofty One, the Holy One. We rejoice in the infilling of your power and joy, Your love and faith. Right now, we receive all that You have to give! By Your grace and mercy, You will once again fill us. Thank You, Lord! Amen.

YOUR MUSINGS

24

Sheep Dip

IN THE SPIRIT

A lone black sheep was scampering down a road and across a small bridge that arched over a clear pool. The animal slipped and fell into the water below. In an instant, what looked like a small pond or creek turned into a water trough, one that you'd see on a farm. A rancher began giving the black sheep and many other sheep baths in this water. I realized it was a sheep dip. (Note: A sheep dip is a liquid formulation of insecticide and fungicide that shepherds and farmers use to protect their sheep against infestation from external parasites, mites, ticks, and lice.)

Though the sheep all went in to the water dirty and bug-infested, they came out clean and whiter than snow. I heard the words, "It's time for a cleansing, but it is not time for a shearing."

IN THE WORD

Deuteronomy 8:7, NLT
For the Lord your God is bringing you into a good land of flowing streams and pools of water . . . .

Psalm 78:52, NKJV
But He made His own people go forth like sheep, And guided them in the wilderness like a flock.

Isaiah 4:4, NLT
The Lord will wash the filth from beautiful Zion and cleanse Jerusalem of its bloodstains . . .

Ezekiel 34:15, NLT
"I myself will tend my sheep and give them a place to lie down in peace," says the Sovereign Lord.

Malachi 3:11, NLT
our crops will be abundant, for I will guard them from insects and disease . . .

Luke 11:2, TPT
. . . Our heavenly Father, may the glory of your name be the center on which our life turns. May your Holy Spirit come upon us and cleanse us. Manifest your kingdom on earth.

John 9: 7, KJV

And He said unto him, Go, wash in the pool of Siloam, (which is by interpretation, Sent.) He went his way therefore, and washed, and came seeing.

1 Peter 2:25, NKJV

For you were like sheep going astray, but have now returned to the Shepherd and Overseer of your souls.

1 Peter 5:2, NLT

Care for the flock that God has entrusted to you Watch over it willingly . . .

· · · · ·

PRAYER

Lord, Your word is so clear! It's time for a cleansing of Your people. We must ready ourselves to be washed by Your hand, by Your Holy Spirit. We are Your sheep and You are a good God, watching over Your flock. We yield to You as our God. As we surrender to You, give us a touch of heaven. Give us a touch of Your grace! We know that in Your cleansing, there is healing. Knowing that a dip into Your Spirit will wash away all uncleanness, all pesky hindrances, we say, "Yes, Lord!" Release that healing upon us, Your people. Cleanse us, heal us, and fill us! Amen.

25

Picket Fence

IN THE SPIRIT

I saw a man was standing in front of a white picket fence, looking for a way to get to the other side. From his perspective, all he could see was a fence on the right, as far as the eye could see, and a fence on the left, also as far as the eye could see. He stood close to it, trying to reach over, but it was much too high. He was stuck! There was no way in!

He then moved to a new location at the fence and saw before him a gate latch. As he opened the now obvious gate (*How did I not see that before?* he wondered to himself), he walked forward, unstuck, and reached the other side.

IN THE WORD

Numbers 22:24, NKJV
Then the Angel of the Lord stood in a narrow path between the vineyards, with a wall on this side and a wall on that side.

Deuteronomy 3:25, NLT
Please let me cross the Jordan to see the wonderful land on the other side, the beautiful hill country and the Lebanon mountains.

Proverbs 15:19, NLT
A lazy person's way is blocked with briers, but the path of the upright is an open highway.

Ecclesiastes 8:6, NLT
For there is a time and a way for everything, even when a person is in trouble.

Isaiah 26:2, NLT
Open the gates to all who are righteous; allow the faithful to enter.

Jeremiah 25:35, NLT
You will find no place to hide; there will be no way to escape.

1 Corinthians 9:20, TPT

. . . I became like one under the law to gain the people who were stuck under the law, even though I myself am not under the law.

. . . . . .

PRAYER

I can see it, I can almost taste it, but I'm just not there yet. I need a way of escape or a place to hide. I'm stuck! I'm in trouble! Yet I remember, You say that You are my hiding place. You are my Way and in Your perfect time I will get to the other side. I'm not lazy; in fact, I am victorious and upright. You are my deliverer! All of those who oppose me, I stop you now. I walk in the Truth! Lord, let me cross over to Your wonderful land on the other side. Open the gates because I am upright and righteous. Have Your way with me and give me that special touch from heaven. Thank You, faithful Lord. Amen.

YOUR MUSINGS

26

Puzzle

IN THE SPIRIT

A giant puzzle comprised of large pieces lay across a structure that looked like the foundation of a house. The picture on the puzzle was of a grapevine and an enormous cluster of grapes. In the middle of the cluster, just down from the largest grape, a puzzle piece was falling off. Someone put the puzzle piece back into place, yet the picture was only whole momentarily. Again and again, the piece would fall off and the puzzle would not be complete.

I noticed there was a fissure in the foundation wall of the structure on which the puzzle rested. Next to it was a hole where the puzzle piece had been falling through. In that spot, there was no support in place, just a weak, broken foundation with nothing underneath. There were smears of concrete on the hole, obviously showing that it had been patched many times.

From the side, I saw a hand take a pair of tongs and use them to drop hot coal against the crack in the foundation. Continuously, more coals were dropped in place and a heap formed. Again, the foundation gave way.

I reflected, and felt God speak to me about this vision:

"Until the foundation is remedied, the same cycle will continue."

"What is the cause? Where is the weakness?" I asked.

"It is in the foundation of the structure. The realm of darkness knows where the breach is and how to make it break, over and over again. Pressure at this point becomes unbearable, causing things to crumble once again."

God says, "I am shining My light. It's time to make sure your foundation. Your grape cluster will be made whole. You will be as fruitful as I have said, no longer underscored by things, people, and situations that have taken you apart. No longer will my people be scattered. No longer will fruit dry on the vine. No longer will you be destroyed by him who has continually bombarded you with cunning tactics and maneuvers."

IN THE WORD

Isaiah 30:26, KJV
Moreover the light of the moon shall be as the light of the sun, and the light of the sun shall be sevenfold, as the light of seven days, in the day that the Lord bindeth up the breach of His people., and healeth the stroke of their wound.

Isaiah 58:12, KJV
And they that shall be of thee shall build the old waste places, thou shalt raise up the foundations of many generations and thou shalt be called, the repairer of the breach, the restorer of paths to dwell in.

Isaiah 65:8, KJV
Thus saith the Lord, as the new wine is found in the cluster, and one saith, destroy it not, for a blessing is in it. So will I do for My servant's sake. That I may not destroy them all.

Psalm 107:37, NKJV
And sow fields and plant vineyards, that they may yield a fruitful harvest.

Song of Songs 2:13, KJV
The fig tree putteth forth her green figs, and the vines with the tender grape give a good smell. Arise, my love, My fair one, and come away.

Luke 11:24-26, NLT

When an evil spirit leaves a person, it goes into the desert, searching for rest. But when it finds none, it says, "I will return to the person I came from." So it returns and finds that its former home is all swept and in order. Then the spirit finds seven other spirits more evil than itself, and they all enter the person and live there. And so that person is worse off than before.

· · · · ·

PRAYER

Though there are no grapes on the vine, yet we will praise You. We wrestle to produce good fruit and be fruitful. We search for faults in ourselves that may be open doors for approach. We need You, Lord, to open our eyes to the breaches in our foundations. Look on us, oh God! You are the restorer of the broken and You know all that is within us. We surrender to You and Your cleansing hand. We want to be like You. Cleanse us, and we will be clean. Make us fully fruitful, full of good fruit that can't be taken. Fill us, Lord, with Your Spirit, and bless us. Amen.

27

Sandcastle

IN THE SPIRIT

I saw a woman walk into a sandcastle that was the size of a large mansion. As she walked through the oversized front door, I sensed intense worries and cares overwhelming her. She continued to walk through the collapsing sandcastle as she strained to see what was outside the open back door, a door much smaller than the front door.

She dodged the obstacles that got in her way as she made her way to the door. From that doorway, she saw a narrow pathway winding up and around a high, peaked mountain. She made her way toward it, then struggled to slowly climb it until she reached the top of the mountain. At the pinnacle of the mountain, she heard a voice telling her, "You have been visiting the sandcastle of the 'non-essential.'"

I sensed the Lord showing me that I, too, had been visiting the "sandcastle of the non-essential." I realized there was an open door into this manmade castle, inviting me into worries about my family, work, health, and relationships. These worries had confined me within the walls of this sinking, unstable structure.

I felt the Lord telling me that Jesus was calling me out, asking me to leave my cares behind. "Come away with Me to the pinnacle of what is best for you!" He urged me.

I sensed Him beckoning me to leave the sinking sand. "I'll show you the way," He said. "It's narrow and winding and will take effort on your part. However, I have called you to the peak of the mountain. Build your life on the rock, not on the sand. The call has been made on your life into a high, greater, and more profound journey. Come away from this sandcastle and I will lead you."

IN THE WORD

Song of Songs 2:14, TPT
"There is a change in the air." Arise, My love, My beautiful companion, and run with Me to a higher place. For now is the time to arise and come away with Me.

Matthew 7:13-14, TPT
Come to God through the narrow gate, because the wide gate and broad path is the way that leads to destruction-nearly everyone chooses the crowded road. The narrow gate and the difficult way leads to eternal life, so few ever find it.

Matthew 7:26, TPT
But everyone who hears My teachings and does not apply it to his life can be compared to a foolish man who built his life on the sand.

Mark 4:18-19, TPT
The seed that fell among the thorns represents others who hear God's word, but all too quickly the message is crowded out by the worries of this life, the lure of wealth, and the desire for other things, so no fruit is produced.

PRAYER

Father, take us by the hand and lead us out of shifting sandy structures, which are so deceptive. They offer us no protection or solace.

You have saved us from being subject to the cares of this world by paving and leading the way into Your presence. Thank You for calling me. I choose to come away with You. I am willing to pay the price and the sacrifice of obedience. My higher place is only with You.

You have made the way and I choose to follow! I want to live in my high calling. I want to be filled with a love for You that no circumstance can take away. Reveal Yourself to me in ways only You can do. Amen.

28

The Big Game

IN THE SPIRIT

I saw a man playing football, dressed in football gear and holding a deflated leather football with the lacing facing out. The ball was deflated and he pressed it against his body as he backed away from the football field.

Suddenly, the other players on the field seized the player and began tossing him about like a rag doll, moving towards the wrong end zone. They placed him flat on his back in the middle of the playing field. The announcer sounded, "Illegal hit! It's a foul!"

Just then, a strong wind kicked up and blew on the player, raising him up and re-inflating the ball. He was reinvigorated and began racing toward his own end zone. He ran ahead of all the players who had tackled him to the ground, and left their defense in the dust.

The cheerleaders cheered and the crowd screamed as he gained more and more yards. *Touchdown!*

Upon reflection, I realized that many of us have been in the role of the "player." Some have been hit by the snare of the fowler (fouler), and have had the wind knocked out of them; some have been knocked out of bounds, fouled by others. Positions of comfort, security, honor, and pleasure have been stolen from some as they were tossed into the wrong end zone.

I sensed God saying, "I am here to breathe again into you my Spirit breath, to quicken your spirit and put you back in the game. Because the fowler (fouler) came against you, I will advance you for each blow struck against you. The violently determined shall take that which was taken from them and more. You will see yourself move into the greater things that you have desired and I will restore your soul, and your emotional and spiritual well-being, many times over."

. . . . .

IN THE WORD

2 Timothy 4:7, KJV
I have fought the good fight, I have finished the race, I have kept the faith.

Psalm 35:2, TPT

Put on your armor, Lord; take up your shield and protect me. Rise up, mighty God! Grab your weapons of war and block the way of the wicked who come to fight me. Stand for me when they stand against me! Speak over my soul: "I am your strong Savior!"

Psalm 91:3, KJV

Surely, He shall deliver you from the snare of the fowler and from the perilous pestilence.

Matthew 11:12, NKJV

And from the days of John the Baptist until now the kingdom of heaven suffers violence, and the violent take it by force.

John 10:10, NKJV

The thief does not come except to steal, and to kill, and to destroy. I have come that they may have life, and that they may have it more abundantly.

1 Corinthians 9:25, NKJV

And everyone who competes for the prize is temperate in all things. Now they do it to obtain a perishable crown, but we for an imperishable crown.

Philippians 3:14, NKJV

I press toward the goal for the prize of the upward call of God in Christ Jesus.

2 Timothy 2:5, NKJV

And also if anyone competes in athletics, he is not crowned unless he competes according to the rules.

Hebrews 12:1, NLT

Therefore, since we are surrounded by such a huge crowd of witnesses to the life of faith, let us strip off every weight that slows us down, especially the sin that so easily trips us up. And let us run with endurance the race God has set before us.

. . . . .

PRAYER

Here I go again, fighting the good fight! Lord, You are always here to guide me and protect me. I thank You for Your care, but right now I am pleading for the grace to be the one who takes it by force. It's only by Your empowerment that I will arise victorious. I have caught the fowler and I declare, "No more, not this time!" I am pressing forward, no matter what, again, by Your grace. I set my eyes on the prize of Your high call. I will not be shaken. I ask for greater passion, for greater grace. Right now, I celebrate You, my Victor! Amen.

29

Storm

IN THE SPIRIT

I was standing on a hill, overlooking a town in the valley below. As I looked down, I saw a dark storm taking shape in the distance. It rumbled and crashed with flashes of lightning as it moved closer and closer toward me.

As I watched, a man came and stood next to me. He put his arm around me as we sat down together on the grass, watching the storm grow as it approached. He asked me if I was afraid. I knew I was, but didn't want to admit it.

"You can do something about this," he said to me. "Weren't you told to pray about everything?" At that moment I knew Who He was and what I needed to do. I prayed like I owned the world, with all the authority that is in the name of Jesus. The storm passed overhead as I sat in His comfort. I didn't feel any wind, nor even a drop of rain.

As I mused over this vision, I heard a voice speak to me, saying, "A storm is coming, but I will comfort you. Speak to the storm. Don't just watch it. Call forth the hosts of heaven's armies to ward off all works of darkness from you or your family and loved ones."

· · · · ·

IN THE WORD

Deuteronomy 32:10, MSG
He found him out in the wilderness, in an empty, windswept wasteland. He threw his arms around him, lavished attention on him, guarding him as the apple of his eye . . .

Psalm 55:8, TPT
I will hurry off to hide in the higher place, into my shelter, safe from this raging storm and tempest.

Psalm 107:29, TPT
God stilled the storm, calmed the waves, and he hushed the hurricane winds to only a whisper.

Jeremiah 1:19, NLT
They will fight you, but they will fail. For I am with you, and I will take care of you. I, the Lord have spoken.

John 14:14, TPT

Ask me for anything in my name, and I will do it for you!"

Mark 4:37,39, NKJV

And a great windstorm arose . . . Then He arose and rebuked the wind, and said to the sea, "Peace, be still!" And the wind ceased and there was a great calm.

Luke 10:17, NKJV

"Lord, even the demons are subject to us in Your name."

. . . . . .

PRAYER

You instruct me in my sleep. You teach me Your ways in the night. Lord, I am so thankful for the comfort You give and the power You bestow in Your mighty name. You say, "No weapon that is formed against me will be prosperous." The storm of life that came to derail me is under Your authority as I release Your name, Jesus! I will not fear! You take me to a higher place. You are my shelter. As You have given me Your authority, I exercise my privilege. "Storm, be still! I call a halt to the assignments against me. Go to the feet of Jesus!" Your peace has come to me because of Who You are. Thank You. Amen.

30

Fan

IN THE SPIRIT

A congregation of people were seated in a large room. Each had an Asian-style fan made of paper, and they were fanning themselves. They seemed overwhelmed by waves of heat, like someone might feel when they've had a sudden "hot flash."

As they fanned themselves, the people seemed to feel relief from the moving air, and appeared comfortable and content. They were feeling a small breeze from the movement of the fan, and they thought contentedly, "This is the wind of the Spirit." Each person imagined they were in the flow of all God had to offer, that it was enough to fulfill them and keep them. Their self-made breeze was small, but they were comfortable.

Then a voice spoke, saying, "I want to blow on this people with a blast of my Spirit wind! Like I promised,

I have more for you. There is more!" The eyes of each person widened as they heard the voice and considered that there might be more for them than what they were used to, and what they thought was enough.

......

IN THE WORD

Psalm 85:7, TPT

Pour out even more of your love on us! Reveal more of your kindness and restore us back to you!

Song of Songs 4:16, NLT

Awake, north wind! Rise up, south wind! . . .

Joel 2:29, NLT

In those days I will pour out my Spirit even on servants— men and women alike.

John 3:8, TPT

For the Spirit-wind blows as it chooses. You can hear its sound, but you don't know where it came from or where it's going. So it is within the hearts of those who are Spirit-born!

Acts 2:2, TPT

Suddenly they heard the sound of a violent blast of wind rushing into the house from out of the heavenly realm. The roar of the wind was so overpowering it was all anyone could bear!

2 Timothy 1:6, TPT

I'm writing to encourage you to fan into a flame and rekindle the fire of the spiritual gift God imparted to you when I laid my hands upon you.

· · · · ·

PRAYER

It's as simple as this: call for the wind of the Spirit. "Awake, rise up," we cry out. Lord, forgive us for being content with only a little breeze of Your Spirit. Awaken us to know that there is so much more for us. Awaken us to ask You for more. So, we call out. More, Lord! Pour out an increase of Your Spirit upon and in us! Teach us how to fan the Spirit into flame. How can we be constantly filled with You? Blow on us Lord! We receive what You impart. Thank You, Lord. Amen.

YOUR MUSINGS

31

Scope

IN THE SPIRIT

Looking through the scope of a rifle, my sights were set on finding the perfect trophy for my hunting efforts. I saw many unusual creatures running across my field of vision. I knew I would know when just the right prize was before me. At that point, I would take it.

Then, almost instantly, I saw it, perfect in every way. It presented itself to me in ultimate vulnerability. I made corrections to the cross hairs on the scope. This was my target; this was my prize! I took my shot—I felt like an amateur sharpshooter. But just after I did, I saw it—a sign that read "No Poaching."

IN THE WORD

Psalm 25:8, MSG
God is fair and just; He corrects the misdirected, and sends them in the right direction.

Psalm 119:137, MSG
You are right and you do right, God; your decisions are right on target.

Acts 13:39, NLT
Everyone who believes in Him is made right in God's sight—something the law of Moses could never do.

Ephesians 5:13, TPT
Whatever the revelation-light exposes, it will also correct, and everything that reveals truth is light to the soul.

Philippians 1:6, TPT
I pray with great faith for you, because I'm fully convinced that the One who began this glorious work in you will faithfully continue the process of maturing you and will put his finishing touches to it until the unveiling of our Lord Jesus Christ.

Colossians 3:1, NLT

Since you have been raised to new life with Christ, set you sights on the realities of heaven, where Christ sits in the place of honor at God's right hand.

2 Timothy 2:5, TPT

An athlete who doesn't play by the rules will never receive the trophy, so remain faithful to God.

2 Timothy 4:8, NLT

And now the prize awaits me—the crown of righteousness, which the Lord, the righteous Judge, will give me on the day of his return. And the prize is not just for me but for all who eagerly look forward to his appearing.

1 Thessalonians 2:19, TPT

For what will be our confident hope, our exhilaration joy, or our wonderful trophy that we will boast in before our Lord Jesus at his appearing? It is you!

PRAYER

I set my sights on You, Lord. Though many creatures pass before me, they are not my prize, You are! You have exposed Yourself with revelation light and I see that my trophy is You. Keep my ways true, Lord, and my aim steady as I pursue You. You are my hope and joy and I boast in You. Correct me and align my cross hairs so that I don't miss the mark. Make corrections in me that lead me to a place of accuracy in the things of the Spirit. Use me, Lord, to bless others as You have blessed me. Amen.

About the Author

Carol M. BoRich has been a follower of Jesus since 1975. She has a passion for prayer, intercession, and prophetic ministry, and is currently a member of the prayer ministry team at her local church. She is a frequent speaker and prophetic minister to Christian groups and gatherings.

Carol also has a heart for ministry for women, and serves as a women's small group leader, mentor, and minister at the Washington Corrections Center for Women. For many years, she was part of Women's Aglow, and served as honorary president and speaker.

Carol is a homeschool mother of two children and nanny to two of her eight grandchildren. She and her husband Bob make their home in Gig Harbor, Washington.

Contact

Thank you for musing with me.
I invite your personal revelation.
Feel free to contact me and
share your own reflections
through my website at
www.BoRichMinistries.com.

www.ingramcontent.com/pod-product-compliance
Lightning Source LLC
Chambersburg PA
CBHW042115100526
44587CB00025B/4059